SUPERHERO SCIENCE

HEROES of LIGHT and SOUND

JOY LIN

ILLUSTRATED BY
ALAN BROWN

B.E.S.
PUBLISHING

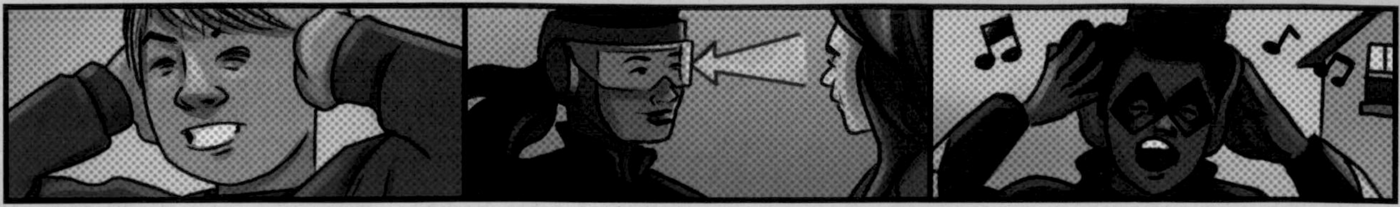

FIRST EDITION FOR THE UNITED STATES, ITS TERRITORIES AND DEPENDENCIES, THE PHILIPPINE REPUBLIC, AND CANADA PUBLISHED IN 2019 BY B.E.S. PUBLISHING CO.

FIRST PUBLISHED IN GREAT BRITAIN IN 2018 BY WAYLAND, AN IMPRINT OF HACHETTE CHILDREN'S GROUP, PART OF HODDER & STOUGHTON.

ALL INQUIRIES SHOULD BE ADDRESSED TO:
B.E.S. PUBLISHING CO.
250 WIRELESS BOULEVARD
HAUPPAUGE, NY 11788
WWW.BES-PUBLISHING.COM

ISBN: 978-1-4380-1266-7

LIBRARY OF CONGRESS CONTROL NUMBER: 2018951833

DATE OF MANUFACTURE: JANUARY 2019
MANUFACTURED BY: WKT, SHENZHEN, CHINA

PRINTED IN CHINA
9 8 7 6 5 4 3 2 1

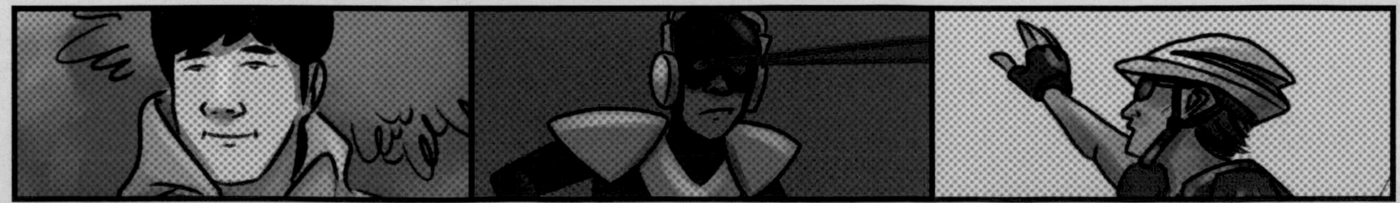

What if I had a superpower?

HAVEN'T WE ALL ASKED OURSELVES THIS QUESTION AT SOME POINT? IT WOULD BE AMAZING TO BE INVISIBLE, HAVE X-RAY VISION, SUPER HEARING, OR A SONIC SCREAM. ARE THESE ABILITIES THE STUFF OF DREAMS OR WILL WE ONE DAY BE ABLE TO BE REAL-LIFE SUPERHEROES?

ONCE UPON A TIME WE WERE ONLY ABLE TO OBSERVE THE STARS FROM EARTH AND DREAM OF EXPLORING SPACE, THEN ONE DAY, WE SENT MEN TO THE MOON! SCIENCE IS DEFINITELY CATCHING UP WITH OUR IMAGINATIONS. LET'S SEE WHAT HAPPENS WHEN YOU APPLY THE LAWS OF SCIENCE TO SUPERPOWERS . . .

CONTENTS

HOW DO OUR EYES AND EARS WORK?

Light and sound make it possible to see and hear. Almost everything we do involves our eyes and ears. So let's start by going over how our eyes work.

I CAN'T SEE ANYTHING!

IF A ROOM IS COMPLETELY PITCH BLACK, YOU WILL NOT BE ABLE TO SEE ANYTHING AT ALL EVEN IF YOUR EYES ARE WIDE OPEN. TRY LOOKING AT YOUR HAND AFTER TURNING OFF THE LIGHTS IN A WINDOWLESS ROOM.

1. IN ORDER FOR YOU TO SEE AN OBJECT, FIRST THERE NEEDS TO BE A LIGHT SOURCE, NO MATTER HOW FAINT. THE LIGHT RAYS HIT THE OBJECT AND REFLECT OFF IT INTO YOUR EYE THROUGH THE **CORNEA**.

2. THE CORNEA BENDS THE LIGHT RAYS, WHICH THEN PASS THROUGH THE **PUPIL**. DUE TO THE WAY THE LIGHT PASSES INTO THE EYE, THE IMAGE IS PROJECTED ONTO THE RETINA UPSIDE DOWN AND REVERSED.

3. THE **IRIS**, WHICH SURROUNDS THE PUPIL, ADJUSTS ITS SIZE AROUND THE PUPIL ACCORDING TO THE AMOUNT OF LIGHT THERE IS. THIS IS WHY OUR PUPILS APPEAR SMALLER IN THE SUNSHINE AND BIGGER WHEN IT IS DARK.

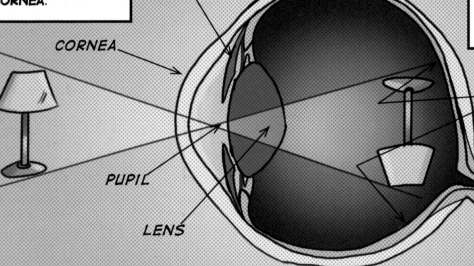

IRIS

CORNEA

PUPIL

LENS

RETINA

OPTIC NERVE

4. THE LIGHT RAYS PASS THROUGH THE **LENS** NEXT, WHICH IS CLEAR AND COLORLESS. ITS JOB IS TO FOCUS THE LIGHT RAYS ON THE RETINA.

5. THE **RETINA** CONTAINS NERVE CELLS CALLED RODS AND CONES. THE RODS HELP US SEE LIGHT AND DARK, AND THE CONES SENSE ONE OF THREE DIFFERENT COLORS (GREEN, RED, OR BLUE). TOGETHER, CONES CAN SENSE COMBINATIONS OF COLORS. THE RODS AND CONES PROCESS AND CONVERT THE LIGHT RAYS INTO NERVE MESSAGES.

6. THE NERVE MESSAGES ARE SENT TO THE BRAIN VIA THE **OPTIC NERVE**. THEN THE BRAIN "FIXES" THE UPSIDE DOWN AND REVERSED IMAGE AND INTERPRETS WHAT IT IS YOU ARE SEEING.

Now, let's go over how our ears work.

SOUND IS PRODUCED WHEN SOMETHING VIBRATES ENOUGH TO CAUSE THE AIR AROUND IT TO VIBRATE IN ALL DIRECTIONS, LIKE A RIPPLE. THESE SOUND WAVES THEN REACH YOUR OUTER EAR, WHERE THEY ARE COLLECTED AND SENT DOWN THROUGH THE **EAR CANAL**.

WHEN THE SOUND WAVES PASS FROM THE EAR CANAL THROUGH TO THE **EARDRUM**, THEY MAKE IT VIBRATE. THE VIBRATIONS MOVE THREE DELICATE BONES IN THE MIDDLE EAR ONE AFTER ANOTHER. THEY ARE CALLED THE OSSICLES. THEY AMPLIFY THE SOUND.

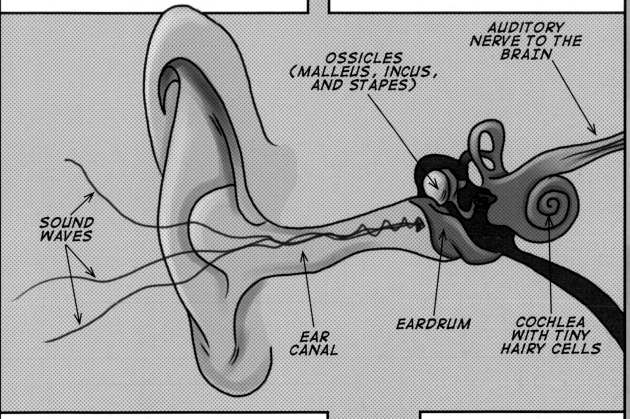

OSSICLES (MALLEUS, INCUS, AND STAPES)

AUDITORY NERVE TO THE BRAIN

SOUND WAVES

EAR CANAL

EARDRUM

COCHLEA WITH TINY HAIRY CELLS

NEXT STOP FOR THE VIBRATIONS IS THE **COCHLEA** IN YOUR INNER EAR, WHICH IS FILLED WITH LIQUID AND LINED WITH TINY CELLS WITH HAIRS. THE VIBRATIONS CAUSE THESE HAIRS TO MOVE, SENDING NERVE MESSAGES TO THE BRAIN VIA THE AUDITORY NERVE.

THE BRAIN THEN INTERPRETS THE VIBRATIONS AS SOUNDS AND SEARCHES THROUGH ITS MEMORIES TO RECOGNIZE WHAT THE SOUND IS.

THAT IS HOW YOU ARE ABLE TO SEE AND HEAR. IT SEEMS LIKE A LOT OF STEPS, BUT SOUND WAVES TRAVEL AT ABOUT 1,000 FT (340 M) PER SECOND AND LIGHT TRAVELS AT AN ASTONISHING ALMOST 190,000 (300,000,000 M) PER SECOND, SO OUR PERCEPTION OF SOUND AND IMAGE IS ALMOST INSTANT. BUT IT IS POSSIBLE TO NOTICE THE DIFFERENCE IN THE SPEED OF LIGHT AND SOUND DURING A THUNDERSTORM. THE SAME EVENT CAUSES BOTH THUNDER AND LIGHTNING, BUT THE DIFFERENCE IN THEIR SPEED IS WHY WE SEE THE LIGHTNING FIRST AND HEAR THE THUNDER SECOND.

Now, let's see what happens when we apply the science of sound and vision to superpowers.

Mr. INVISIBLE: HAS HE EVER BEEN SEEN?

How cool would it be to be an invisible superhero? You could listen in on bad guys' plans and conversations without them knowing you were there.

FIRST WE'LL BREAK DOWN THE DOOR.

YEAH, THEN WE FIND THE SAFE.

YOU'D BE ABLE TO TAKE BACK STOLEN JEWELRY AND MONEY FROM THIEVES AND ROBBERS!

BUT BEFORE YOU GET TOO EXCITED ABOUT YOUR NEW POWER, THERE ARE A FEW THINGS YOU SHOULD CONSIDER.

MR. INVISIBLE'S SUPERPOWERS
- to be invisible from the inside out
- great for spying on the enemy

FIRST OF ALL, A FLOATING HOODIE AND TROUSERS WOULD SCARE LOTS OF PEOPLE, SO GUESS WHAT YOU'VE GOT TO DO? THAT'S RIGHT, BETTER START STRIPPING UNTIL YOU'RE COMPLETELY NAKED.

YOU ALSO CAN'T CARRY ANYTHING WITH YOU: NO PHONE, NO MONEY, OR KEYS, NOTHING!

SINCE PEOPLE CAN'T SEE YOU, YOU'VE GOT TO AVOID THEM. ALL OF THEM!

SO COLD!

NEXT, YOU NEED TO WALK ON TIPTOES, AS YOU CANNOT MAKE A SOUND. AND MAKE SURE YOU DON'T HAVE A RUNNY NOSE OR SOMEBODY WILL HEAR YOU SNIFFLING . . .

ALSO, YOU HAVE TO MAKE SURE YOU DON'T SMELL AT ALL (WHETHER IT'S A GOOD SMELL OR NOT) OR YOU'LL BE NOTICED.

NOW IT'S TIME TO RETRIEVE THE STOLEN MONEY FROM THE THIEVES' SAFE. HOW ARE YOU GOING TO DO THAT? YOU COULDN'T BRING ANY TOOLS!

EVEN IF YOU COULD GET TO THE MONEY, A BAG THAT MOVES ON ITS OWN IS GOING TO ATTRACT ATTENTION, TOO.

HEY!

YOU NEED TO STAY SAFE, SO YOU DROP THE BAG. NOW THERE'S NO WAY THEY'LL KNOW WHERE YOU ARE ANY MORE, RIGHT?

WHAT IF IT'S BEEN RAINING AND A CAR SPLASHES A PUDDLE ONTO YOU? THE DIRTY WATER IS NOT INVISIBLE, SO IT WOULD REFLECT LIGHT AND REVEAL YOUR POSITION!

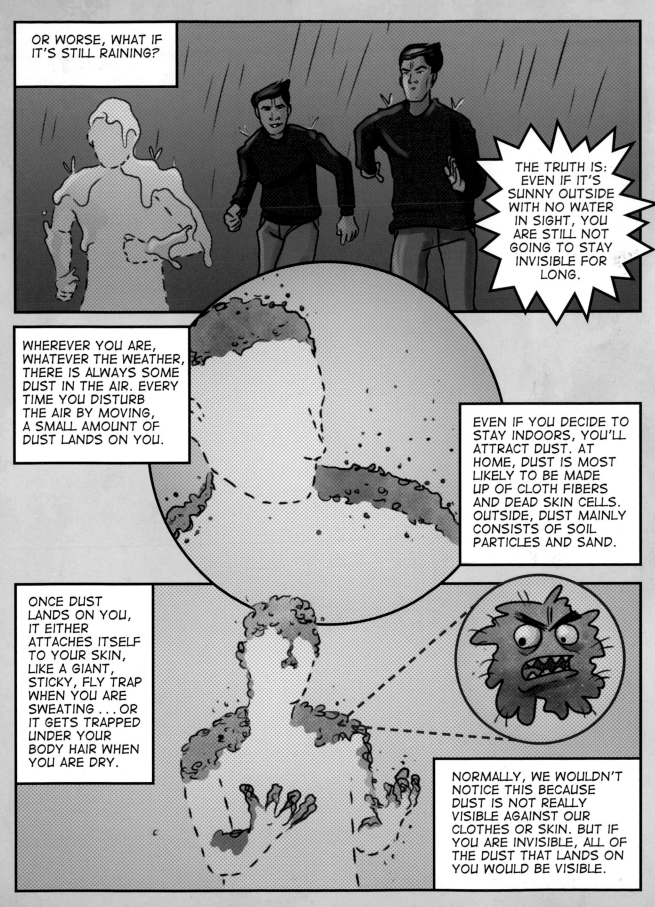

OR WORSE, WHAT IF IT'S STILL RAINING?

THE TRUTH IS: EVEN IF IT'S SUNNY OUTSIDE WITH NO WATER IN SIGHT, YOU ARE STILL NOT GOING TO STAY INVISIBLE FOR LONG.

WHEREVER YOU ARE, WHATEVER THE WEATHER, THERE IS ALWAYS SOME DUST IN THE AIR. EVERY TIME YOU DISTURB THE AIR BY MOVING, A SMALL AMOUNT OF DUST LANDS ON YOU.

EVEN IF YOU DECIDE TO STAY INDOORS, YOU'LL ATTRACT DUST. AT HOME, DUST IS MOST LIKELY TO BE MADE UP OF CLOTH FIBERS AND DEAD SKIN CELLS. OUTSIDE, DUST MAINLY CONSISTS OF SOIL PARTICLES AND SAND.

ONCE DUST LANDS ON YOU, IT EITHER ATTACHES ITSELF TO YOUR SKIN, LIKE A GIANT, STICKY, FLY TRAP WHEN YOU ARE SWEATING . . . OR IT GETS TRAPPED UNDER YOUR BODY HAIR WHEN YOU ARE DRY.

NORMALLY, WE WOULDN'T NOTICE THIS BECAUSE DUST IS NOT REALLY VISIBLE AGAINST OUR CLOTHES OR SKIN. BUT IF YOU ARE INVISIBLE, ALL OF THE DUST THAT LANDS ON YOU WOULD BE VISIBLE.

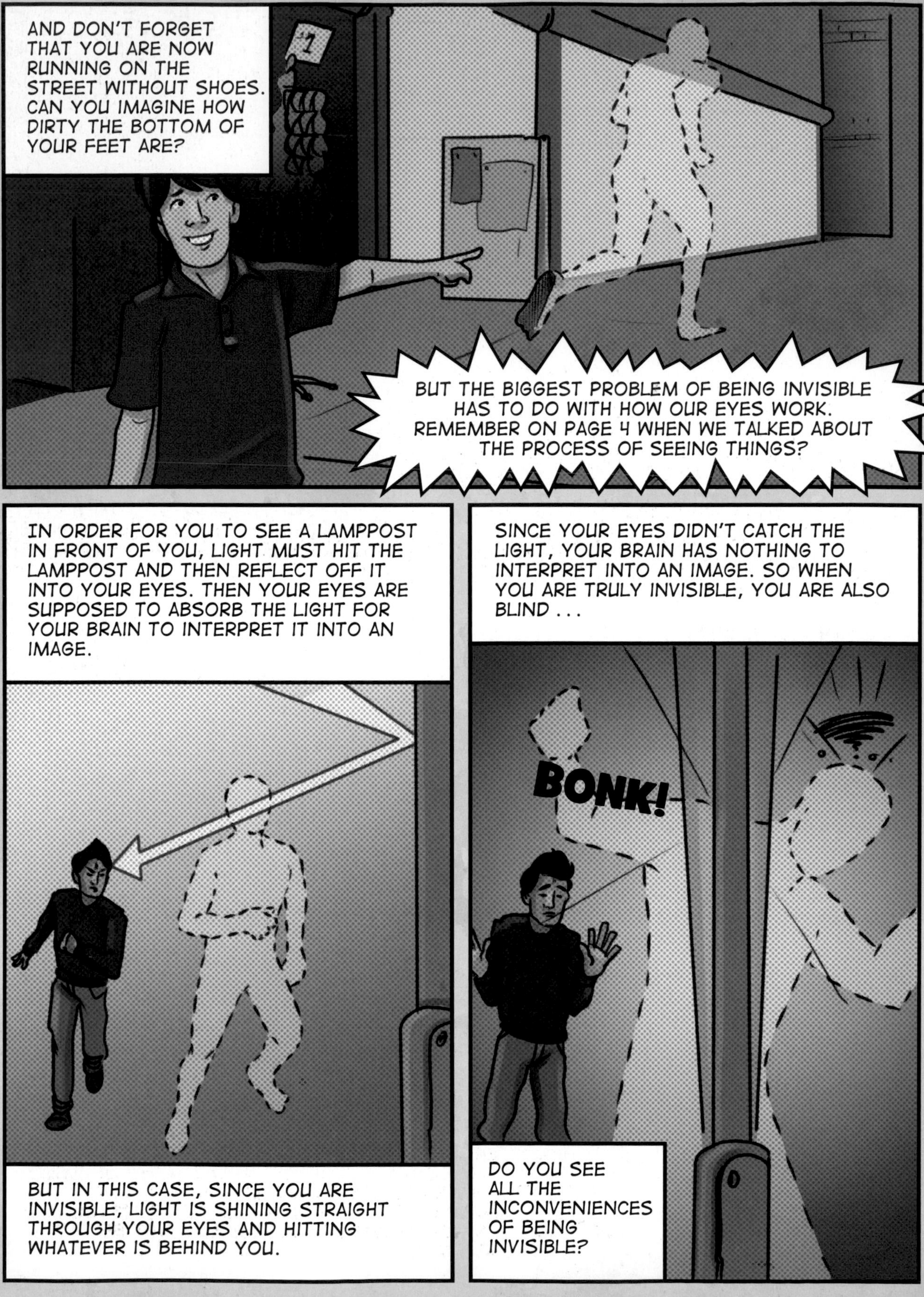
AND DON'T FORGET THAT YOU ARE NOW RUNNING ON THE STREET WITHOUT SHOES. CAN YOU IMAGINE HOW DIRTY THE BOTTOM OF YOUR FEET ARE?
BUT THE BIGGEST PROBLEM OF BEING INVISIBLE HAS TO DO WITH HOW OUR EYES WORK. REMEMBER ON PAGE 4 WHEN WE TALKED ABOUT THE PROCESS OF SEEING THINGS?
IN ORDER FOR YOU TO SEE A LAMPPOST IN FRONT OF YOU, LIGHT MUST HIT THE LAMPPOST AND THEN REFLECT OFF IT INTO YOUR EYES. THEN YOUR EYES ARE SUPPOSED TO ABSORB THE LIGHT FOR YOUR BRAIN TO INTERPRET IT INTO AN IMAGE.
BUT IN THIS CASE, SINCE YOU ARE INVISIBLE, LIGHT IS SHINING STRAIGHT THROUGH YOUR EYES AND HITTING WHATEVER IS BEHIND YOU.
SINCE YOUR EYES DIDN'T CATCH THE LIGHT, YOUR BRAIN HAS NOTHING TO INTERPRET INTO AN IMAGE. SO WHEN YOU ARE TRULY INVISIBLE, YOU ARE ALSO BLIND . . .
BONK!
DO YOU SEE ALL THE INCONVENIENCES OF BEING INVISIBLE?

ALSO, WHAT IF THIS INVISIBILITY IS PERMANENT? HOW IS A DOCTOR GOING TO TREAT THAT BIG BUMP ON YOUR HEAD FROM HITTING THE LAMPPOST IF THEY CAN'T SEE YOU?

HELLO?

EVEN THOUGH MAGICIANS OFTEN USE MIRRORS AND PROPS TO CONVINCE PEOPLE THEY'VE MADE SOMETHING DISAPPEAR, NOBODY CAN REALLY TURN INVISIBLE FROM THE INSIDE OUT.

TA-DAH!

HOWEVER, THERE HAVE BEEN ALL SORTS OF EXCITING ADVANCES IN SCIENCE AND TECHNOLOGY REGARDING INVISIBILITY. SCIENTISTS HAVE FOUND MULTIPLE WAYS TO MANIPULATE LIGHT SO SOMETHING APPEARS TO BE INVISIBLE FROM CERTAIN ANGLES. SOME USE LENSES TO BEND LIGHT TO MAKE OBJECTS APPEAR INVISIBLE, WHILE OTHERS USE SPECIAL MATERIALS THAT HAVE AMAZING OPTICAL PROPERTIES. IT SEEMS LIKE THE DAYS OF INVISIBILITY CLOAKS MAY NOT BE THAT FAR AWAY!

X-RAY IRIS:
THERE'S NOTHING SHE CAN'T SEE!

Wouldn't it be great if you had super vision and X-ray vision?

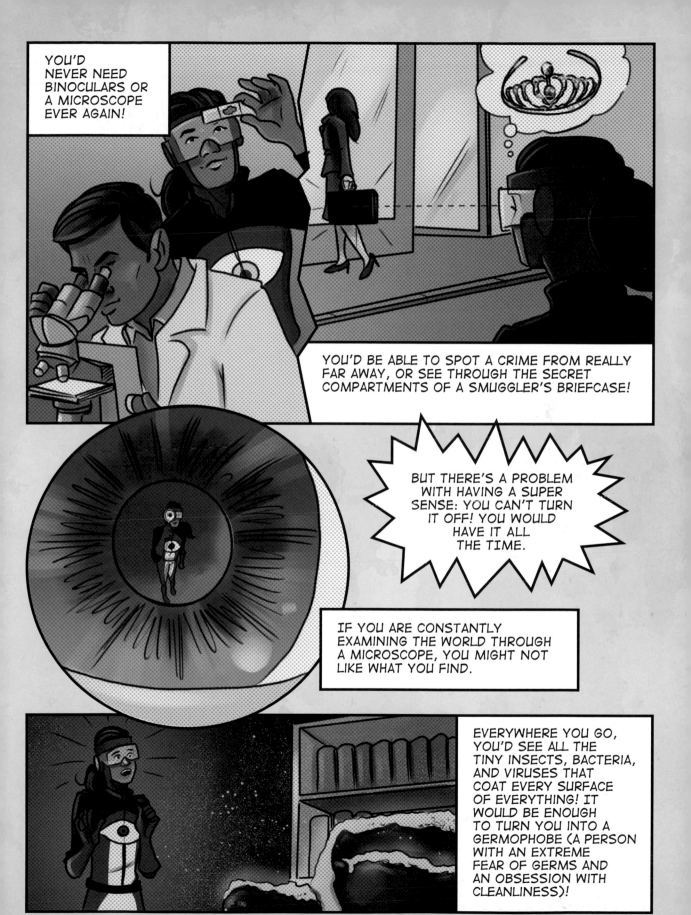

YOU'D NEVER NEED BINOCULARS OR A MICROSCOPE EVER AGAIN!

YOU'D BE ABLE TO SPOT A CRIME FROM REALLY FAR AWAY, OR SEE THROUGH THE SECRET COMPARTMENTS OF A SMUGGLER'S BRIEFCASE!

BUT THERE'S A PROBLEM WITH HAVING A SUPER SENSE: YOU CAN'T TURN IT OFF! YOU WOULD HAVE IT ALL THE TIME.

IF YOU ARE CONSTANTLY EXAMINING THE WORLD THROUGH A MICROSCOPE, YOU MIGHT NOT LIKE WHAT YOU FIND.

EVERYWHERE YOU GO, YOU'D SEE ALL THE TINY INSECTS, BACTERIA, AND VIRUSES THAT COAT EVERY SURFACE OF EVERYTHING! IT WOULD BE ENOUGH TO TURN YOU INTO A GERMOPHOBE (A PERSON WITH AN EXTREME FEAR OF GERMS AND AN OBSESSION WITH CLEANLINESS)!

YOUR PERCEPTION OF COLOR WOULD BE REALLY MESSED UP. MOST COLORS WE SEE ARE A COMBINATION OF THE THREE PRIMARY COLORS OF LIGHT: RED, BLUE, AND GREEN. WHEN YOU COMBINE RED AND BLUE, YOU MAKE MAGENTA; RED AND GREEN TOGETHER MAKE YELLOW; AND MIXING BLUE WITH GREEN IS HOW YOU'D GET THE COLOR CYAN (TURQUOISE). WHITE LIGHT IS THE ADDITION OF ALL THREE COLORS. BLACK OR A COMPLETELY DARK ROOM IS THE ABSENCE OF ALL COLORS OF LIGHT.

IF YOU HAVE SUPER VISION, THE WAY YOU PERCEIVE COLOR WOULD BE LIKE SITTING TOO CLOSE TO AN OLD TELEVISION WITH BIG PIXELS. YOU WOULDN'T SEE THE COMBINATIONS, JUST SEPARATE RED-, BLUE-, AND GREEN-COLORED DOTS. YOU WOULD NEED TO SEE THINGS FROM REALLY FAR AWAY FOR THE COLORS TO MAKE SENSE TO YOU.

OKAY, SO SEEING THINGS IN SO MUCH DETAIL MIGHT NOT ACTUALLY BE HELPFUL TO A SUPERHERO. IN FACT, SEEING ALL THE PARTS COULD MAKE YOU LOSE SIGHT OF THE BIG PICTURE. IT WOULD MEAN INFORMATION OVERLOAD FOR YOUR BRAIN!

BUT WHAT IF YOU HAD X-RAY VISION SO YOU COULD SEE THROUGH PEOPLE AND THINGS?

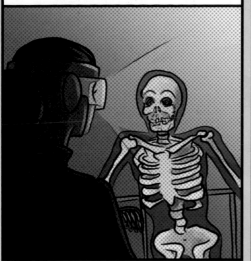

REMEMBER HOW THE HUMAN EYE WORKS? YOU DON'T "SHOOT OUT" EYESIGHT IN ORDER TO SEE A PERSON. INSTEAD, LIGHT BOUNCES OFF THAT PERSON AND THEN ENTERS YOUR EYES. YOUR EYES ARE JUST THE RECEIVERS, NOT THE EMITTERS.

SCIENTISTS DESCRIBE LIGHT AS AN ELECTROMAGNETIC WAVE, WHICH HAS LENGTH AND HEIGHT (JUST LIKE A WAVE IN THE SEA). THE LENGTH OF THE WAVE DETERMINES THE TYPE OF LIGHT COLOR OF THE WAVE. THE HEIGHT EXPRESSES HOW BRIGHT OR INTENSE IT IS. THE HUMAN EYE CAN ONLY SEE A SMALL RANGE OF WAVELENGTHS, WHICH WE CALL VISIBLE LIGHT.

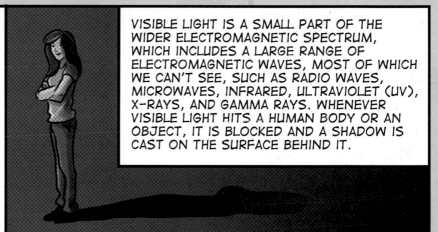

VISIBLE LIGHT IS A SMALL PART OF THE WIDER ELECTROMAGNETIC SPECTRUM, WHICH INCLUDES A LARGE RANGE OF ELECTROMAGNETIC WAVES, MOST OF WHICH WE CAN'T SEE, SUCH AS RADIO WAVES, MICROWAVES, INFRARED, ULTRAVIOLET (UV), X-RAYS, AND GAMMA RAYS. WHENEVER VISIBLE LIGHT HITS A HUMAN BODY OR AN OBJECT, IT IS BLOCKED AND A SHADOW IS CAST ON THE SURFACE BEHIND IT.

X-RAYS ARE SIMILAR TO REGULAR LIGHT RAYS, EXCEPT THEIR WAVELENGTHS ARE A LOT SHORTER, SO THEY INTERACT WITH OBJECTS DIFFERENTLY. MUCH LIKE VISIBLE LIGHT THAT SHINES THROUGH A GLASS WINDOW, X-RAYS PASS THROUGH HUMAN FLESH. BUT X-RAYS DO NOT PASS THROUGH THE DENSER PARTS LIKE HUMAN BONES OR METAL. IT'S A GREAT WAY TO SEE THROUGH HIDDEN COMPARTMENTS AND CATCH A THIEF SMUGGLING JEWELS!

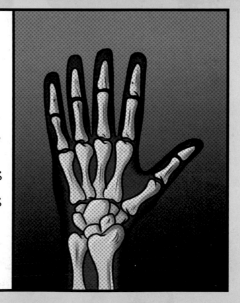

WHEN YOU ARE GIVEN AN X-RAY AT THE HOSPITAL, THEY POINT THE MACHINE AT THE PART OF YOUR BODY THEY ARE TAKING AN X-RAY OF. THERE IS AN X-RAY DETECTOR BEHIND OR IN FRONT OF YOU TO CAPTURE THE X-RAYS IN ORDER TO CREATE AN IMAGE.

IF YOU WERE TO HAVE X-RAY VISION, HOW WOULD THAT WORK? EVEN IF YOU COULD SHOOT X-RAYS OUT OF YOUR EYES TO INSPECT SOMEONE, YOU WOULD NEED AN X-RAY DETECTOR ON THE OTHER SIDE OF THE PERSON IN ORDER TO "SEE" THE IMAGE.

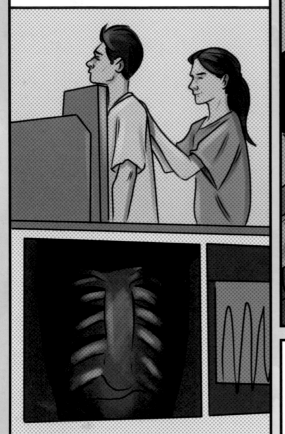

AND LET'S NOT FORGET THAT PROLONGED EXPOSURE TO X-RAY RADIATION CAN BE HARMFUL TO HUMAN BEINGS. SO, IF YOU LIKE THE PERSON YOU ARE LOOKING AT, MAYBE YOU SHOULD STOP LOOKING AT THEM SO YOU DON'T HARM THEM.

YOU'VE BEEN HURTING US WITH YOUR EYES?!?

AND IF **YOU** ARE THE X-RAY DETECTOR, THEN WHERE IS YOUR X-RAY SOURCE? THE SUN EMITS X-RAYS BUT THEY ARE ABSORBED BY THE ATMOSPHERE.

IT SEEMS LIKE HAVING SUPER VISION MIGHT BE MORE OF A PAIN THAN AN AMAZING SUPERPOWER, AND HAVING X-RAY VISION GOES AGAINST HOW OUR EYES ACTUALLY WORK. HOWEVER, VISION-IMPROVING TECHNOLOGY HAS MADE A LOT OF ADVANCES THROUGHOUT THE YEARS—FROM THE INVENTION OF GLASSES, WHICH DATES BACK HUNDREDS OF YEARS, TO MICROSCOPES AND TELESCOPES (BOTH INVENTED IN THE EARLY 17TH CENTURY), AND FROM LASER EYE SURGERY TO CORRECT THE SHAPE OF THE CORNEA AND IMPROVE VISION, TO THE LATEST TELESCOPIC CONTACT LENSES. SCIENTISTS ARE DEFINITELY MAKING THINGS MUCH EASIER FOR US TO SEE.

SUPERHERO:
HE HEARS IT ALL!

What if you had super hearing?

SUPERSONIC'S SUPERPOWERS
- to hear whispers from a long way away
- great for spying on the bad guys

YOU COULD HEAR THE RUMBLE OF A VOLCANO FROM DEEP INSIDE THE EARTH AND WARN EVERYONE.

RUMBLE

RUMBLE

OR HEAR ROBBERS AND THIEVES CREEPING INTO PEOPLE'S HOUSES FROM A LONG WAY AWAY AND TELL THE POLICE.

BUT THE PROBLEM IS, IF YOU HAVE SUPER HEARING, YOU WOULD HAVE IT ALL THE TIME. YOU CANNOT TELL YOUR BRAIN NOT TO HEAR SOMETHING. THIS IS WHY PEOPLE WHO TALK IN MOVIE THEATERS BOTHER US SO MUCH, BECAUSE WE CANNOT "CHOOSE" NOT TO HEAR THEM.

IF YOU WERE ABLE TO HEAR AN OLD LADY BEING ROBBED 10 STREETS AWAY, THAT MEANS YOU WOULD ALSO HEAR EVERY ARGUING COUPLE AND CRYING BABY IN A 10-STREET RADIUS. IN FACT, YOU WOULD BE HEARING SO MUCH NOISE, HER CRIES FOR HELP WOULD BLEND INTO ALL THE TELEVISION AND RADIO PROGRAMS PLAYING NEAR YOU.

WAAAH!

WAAAH!

GROWL!

WOOF! WOOF! WOOF!

BLAH BLAH!

BLAH BLAH!

HELP!

ALSO, YOU COULD ACCIDENTALLY INVADE PEOPLE'S PRIVACY, AND THAT'S NOT GOING TO BE FUN FOR YOU EITHER. DO YOU REALLY WANT TO HEAR ALL YOUR NEIGHBORS' AWFUL SINGING IN THE SHOWER?

IF YOU REALLY HAD SUPER HEARING, YOU WOULD PROBABLY WALK AROUND WEARING EARPLUGS AND NOISE-CANCELING HEADPHONES ALL THE TIME, TRYING TO BLOCK OUT THE INCOMING NOISE.

THIS IS THE SECOND SUPER SENSE THAT TURNS OUT TO BE UNPLEASANT. IN FACT, EVERY SENSE WOULD BECOME UNPLEASANT IF THEY WERE TOO SENSITIVE.

IF YOU HAD SUPER TASTE, FOR INSTANCE, YOU WOULDN'T BE ABLE TO ENJOY NORMAL SEASONED FOODS ANY MORE. BITING INTO A POTATO CHIP WOULD BE LIKE FILLING YOUR MOUTH WITH SEA SALT, AND TAKING A SIP OF FRUIT JUICE WOULD BE LIKE DRINKING CONCENTRATED SYRUP.

AS FOR SMELL, HAVE YOU EVER BEEN TO A PERFUME SHOP AND FELT SO OVERWHELMED BY THE DIFFERENT SCENTS THAT YOU GOT A HEADACHE? IMAGINE THAT MULTIPLIED BY A THOUSAND AND THROW IN SOME UNPLEASANT SMELLS, LIKE ROTTING FOOD, STINKY CHEESE, AND REALLY DIRTY SOCKS ...IT WOULD MAKE YOU FEEL ILL AND PROBABLY DRIVE YOU INSANE!

OKAY, HOW ABOUT TOUCH? IF YOUR SKIN IS EXTRA SENSITIVE TO PLEASURE, IT WOULD ALSO BE EXTRA SENSITIVE TO PAIN. EVEN THE T-SHIRT TAG AT THE BACK OF YOUR NECK WOULD HURT.

I'M EXHAUSTED!

OUCH!

OUR SENSES WORK THE WAY THEY DO FOR A REASON. WE SIMPLY CAN'T HANDLE TOO MUCH OF A GOOD THING.

BUT DID YOU KNOW THAT WHEN WE LOSE A SENSE, SOMETIMES OUR OTHER SENSES ARE HEIGHTENED? THERE ARE A FEW PEOPLE WHO ARE COMPLETELY BLIND, YET THEY CAN GO MOUNTAIN BIKING BY THEMSELVES!

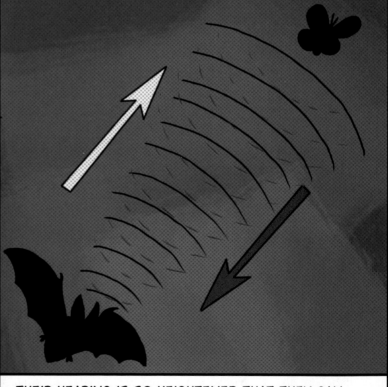

THEIR HEARING IS SO HEIGHTENED THAT THEY CAN USE IT FOR ECHOLOCATION. THEY MAKE A NOISE AND LISTEN FOR THE ECHO. IF THERE IS AN OBJECT RIGHT IN FRONT OF THEM, THE SOUND WAVE WILL BOUNCE BACK IMMEDIATELY. THIS PROCESS IS ALSO HOW BATS ARE ABLE TO "SEE" IN THE DARK TO CATCH INSECTS TO EAT.

THE FURTHER AWAY THE OBJECT IS, THE LONGER IT TAKES FOR THE ECHO TO COME BACK. THE DIFFERENCE IS BARELY NOTICEABLE, BUT THESE AMAZING PEOPLE HAVE TRAINED THEIR EARS SO WELL THAT THEY ARE ABLE TO MAP OUT WHAT IS IN FRONT OF THEM WITHOUT USING THEIR EYES. NOW, THAT IS THE STUFF OF SUPERHEROES!

THE SCREAMIN-- BEAM:

LOOK OUT FOR HER EYES AND VOICE!

What if you could use light and sound as tools or to defend yourself?

SCREAMING BEAM'S SUPERPOWERS

- to shoot lasers out of her eyes to cut through objects
- to scream so loud it incapacitates the enemy

24

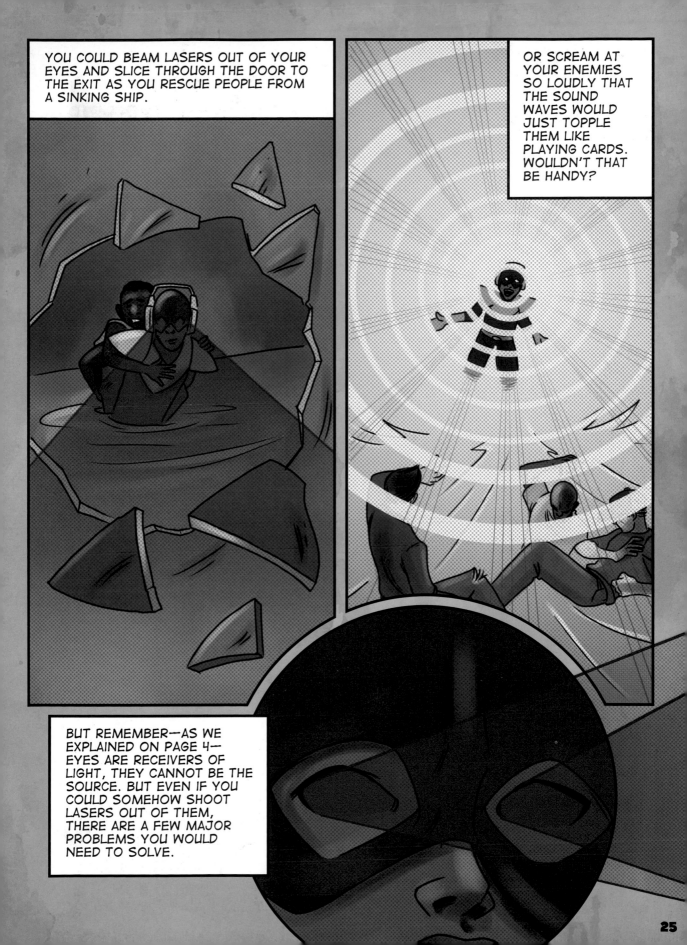

YOU COULD BEAM LASERS OUT OF YOUR EYES AND SLICE THROUGH THE DOOR TO THE EXIT AS YOU RESCUE PEOPLE FROM A SINKING SHIP.

OR SCREAM AT YOUR ENEMIES SO LOUDLY THAT THE SOUND WAVES WOULD JUST TOPPLE THEM LIKE PLAYING CARDS. WOULDN'T THAT BE HANDY?

BUT REMEMBER—AS WE EXPLAINED ON PAGE 4— EYES ARE RECEIVERS OF LIGHT, THEY CANNOT BE THE SOURCE. BUT EVEN IF YOU COULD SOMEHOW SHOOT LASERS OUT OF THEM, THERE ARE A FEW MAJOR PROBLEMS YOU WOULD NEED TO SOLVE.

LET'S SAY YOUR LASER VISION PENETRATES EVERYTHING IN ITS PATH, LIKE A LIGHTSABER, AND YOU CAN TURN IT ON OR OFF AT WILL. YOU MAY NOT UNDERSTAND JUST HOW TERRIBLY DANGEROUS THAT IS.

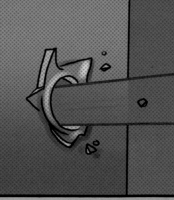

A REGULAR LASER POINTER CAN BE SEEN MORE THAN 2 MI (3 KM) AWAY. IF YOUR LASER VISION HAS HALF OF THAT RANGE, YOU ARE STILL PUTTING ALL THE PEOPLE WITHIN A RADIUS OF 1 MI (1.5 KM) IN DANGER EVERY TIME YOU USE YOUR LASER VISION.

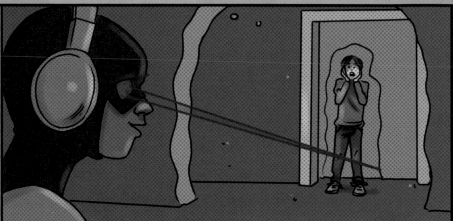

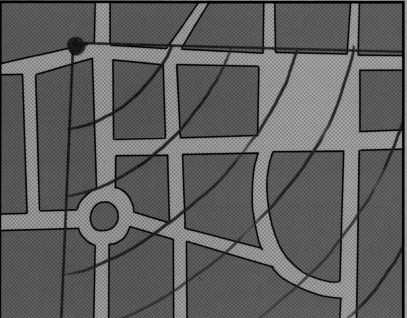

EVEN IF THE RANGE IS ONLY 300 FT (100 M), THAT IS STILL A RIDICULOUS AMOUNT OF POWER FOR DESTRUCTION. BY SIMPLY TURNING YOUR HEAD 90 DEGREES, YOU COULD CUT A DOZEN HOUSES IN HALF (ALONG WITH EVERYONE WHO LIVES IN THEM).

EVEN IF YOU DON'T TURN YOUR HEAD, ACCIDENTS CAN STILL HAPPEN. YOU MAY THINK YOU HAVE STEADY EYESIGHT, BUT YOUR VISION IS ACTUALLY CONSTANTLY MOVING AROUND. THESE SMALL EYE MOVEMENTS ARE CALLED MICROSACCADES AND THEY ARE COMPLETELY INVOLUNTARY.

OOPS!

CAN YOU TELL EXACTLY WHERE THE CENTER OF YOUR VISION IS? THE ANSWER IS NO, YOU CAN'T. MOST OF US HAVE STEREOSCOPIC VISION, WHICH MEANS YOUR PERCEPTION OF WHAT YOU SEE IS A COMBINATION OF TWO SLIGHTLY DIFFERENT IMAGES FROM YOUR TWO EYES. TRY CLOSING ONE EYE AT A TIME AND YOU'LL SEE THE DIFFERENCE.

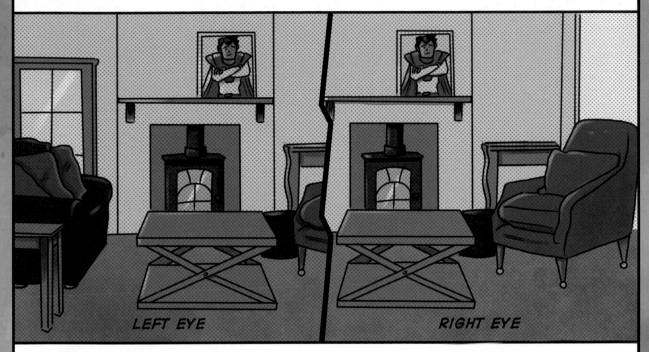

LEFT EYE

RIGHT EYE

THE TWO DIFFERENT ANGLES OF VIEW FROM YOUR EYES ARE CALLED BINOCULAR DISPARITIES. THIS OVERLAPPING PORTION IS PROCESSED IN THE VISUAL CORTEX OF YOUR BRAIN IN ORDER TO GIVE YOU DEPTH PERCEPTION.

SINCE YOUR VISION IS A COMBINED IMAGE FROM TWO EYES, THERE IS NO CENTER OF YOUR VISION. SO HOW WOULD YOU AIM YOUR LASERS AT A TARGET?

IN FACT, IF LASERS ARE SHOOTING OUT OF YOUR RETINAS, THAT MEANS YOUR RETINAS ARE NOT RECEIVING LIGHT FROM THE OUTSIDE. SO WHEN YOU ACTIVATE YOUR LASER VISION, YOU ARE ACTUALLY BLIND WITH NO VISION. NOW, THAT IS JUST RECKLESS ...

AAAH, I CAN'T SEE!

NOW, LET'S SEE WHAT WOULD HAPPEN IF YOU WERE TO USE YOUR SONIC SCREAM TO STOP THE BAD GUYS TRYING TO KIDNAP YOU IN ORDER TO USE YOUR SUPERPOWERS FOR EVIL.

THE ABILITY TO CREATE POWERFUL, SONIC WAVES WITH YOUR VOICE IS ALSO POTENTIALLY HAZARDOUS. FREQUENCIES (NUMBER OF SOUND WAVES OR VIBRATIONS IN A SECOND) ABOVE WHAT HUMAN EARS CAN PICK UP ARE CALLED ULTRASONIC, AND FREQUENCIES BELOW THAT RANGE ARE CALLED INFRASONIC.

I FEEL SICK!

VIBRATIONS WITH ULTRASONIC FREQUENCIES ARE OFTEN REFERRED TO AS ULTRASOUND. EVEN THOUGH HUMANS CANNOT ACTUALLY HEAR ULTRASOUND, HIGH-DECIBEL (THE UNIT USED TO MEASURE THE INTENSITY OF SOUND) ULTRASOUND CAN STILL PERMANENTLY DAMAGE HUMAN EARS. PAST A CERTAIN LEVEL, IT CAN EVEN CAUSE THE HUMAN BODY TO HEAT UP TO HARMFUL LEVELS.

INFRASONIC SOUNDS ARE ALSO UNDETECTABLE BY HUMAN EARS. HOWEVER, THE VIBRATIONS FROM INFRASONIC SOUNDS CAN LEAD TO HEADACHES, DIZZINESS, AND NAUSEA (FEELING SICK).

THE PROBLEM IS THAT SONIC WAVES CANNOT DISTINGUISH THE DIFFERENCE BETWEEN A GOOD GUY AND A BAD GUY. SO EVERY TIME YOU LET OUT A SONIC SCREAM, YOU ARE AFFECTING EVERYONE IN YOUR VICINITY.

BETTER MAKE SURE THERE ARE NO FRIENDS NEARBY BEFORE YOU USE THIS PARTICULAR SUPERPOWER!

SONIC SCREAMS MAY BE THE STUFF OF DREAMS, BUT DIFFERENT KINDS OF SOUND WAVES ARE BEING USED IN NUMEROUS WAYS. FOR EXAMPLE, ULTRASOUND IS USED TO CHECK ON THE HEALTH OF BABIES. ELECTROMAGNETIC WAVES HAVE ALL SORTS OF USES, FROM MICROWAVES TO COOK FOOD, UV LIGHT FOR PURIFYING WATER, AND X-RAYS FOR CHECKING ON BROKEN BONES.

YOUR BABY'S FINE!

ALSO, WE MAY NEVER BE ABLE TO SHOOT LASERS FROM OUR EYES, BUT LASERS ARE USED IN ALL KINDS OF INCREDIBLE WAYS. DOCTORS, FOR EXAMPLE, ARE ABLE TO FOCUS A LASER BEAM TO A MICROSCOPIC DOT WITH VERY HIGH ENERGY DENSITY TO USE IT AS A CUTTING TOOL OR A TOOL THAT STOPS BLEEDING. WHO KNOWS WHAT OTHER USES SCIENTISTS WILL FIND FOR DIFFERENT LIGHT WAVELENGTHS AND SOUND FREQUENCIES?

GLOSSARY

binocular ADAPTED FOR OR USING BOTH EYES TO SEE THINGS

cochlea A SPIRAL-SHAPED TUBE INSIDE THE INNER EAR OF MOST MAMMALS. IT CONTAINS THE NERVE ENDINGS THAT REGISTER SOUND IN THE BRAIN

cornea THE TRANSPARENT, OUTER LAYER THAT COVERS THE FRONT OF THE EYE

decibel THE UNIT USED FOR MEASURING THE LOUDNESS OF SOUND

depth perception THE VISUAL ABILITY TO PERCEIVE THE WORLD IN THREE DIMENSIONS, INCLUDING THE DISTANCE OF OBJECTS IN RELATIONSHIP TO OTHERS

echolocation THE METHOD OF FINDING YOUR WAY OR LOCATING OBJECTS BY PRODUCING A SOUND THAT ECHOES WHEN IT BOUNCES OFF AN OBJECT AND THEN DETERMINING THE TIME AND DIRECTION OF THE ECHO

electromagnetic spectrum THE FULL RANGE OF WAVELENGTHS OF LIGHT, INCLUDING TYPES OF LIGHT HUMANS CAN'T SEE

electromagnetic waves ONE WAY SCIENTISTS DESCRIBE LIGHT IS AS A WAVE. THESE WAVES CAN TRAVEL THROUGH THE EMPTINESS OF SPACE, AT THE SPEED OF LIGHT, CREATING RIPPLES IN ELECTRIC AND MAGNETIC FIELDS

emitter SOMETHING OR SOMEONE THAT SENDS OUT OR GIVES OFF SOMETHING, SUCH AS LIGHT OR NOISE

frequency THE NUMBER OF TIMES THAT A WAVE, ESPECIALLY A LIGHT, SOUND, OR RADIO WAVE, IS PRODUCED WITHIN A PARTICULAR PERIOD, ESPECIALLY ONE SECOND

germ A VERY SMALL ORGANISM THAT CAUSES DISEASE

infrasonic A SOUND TOO LOW FOR HUMANS TO HEAR

iris THE COLORED CIRCLE AROUND THE BLACK PUPIL OF THE EYE

laser A POWERFUL, NARROW BEAM OF LIGHT THAT CAN BE USED AS A TOOL TO CUT METAL, TO PERFORM MEDICAL OPERATIONS, OR TO CREATE PATTERNS OF LIGHT FOR ENTERTAINMENT

lens THE CLEAR PART OF THE EYE THAT BRINGS TOGETHER THE RAYS OF LIGHT NEEDED FOR SIGHT. THE LENS FOCUSES RAYS OF LIGHT SO THAT THEY FORM AN IMAGE INSIDE THE EYE ON THE RETINA

microsaccade A SMALL, JERKY EYE MOVEMENT THAT IS A PART OF NORMAL VISION WHEN FOCUSING ON AN IMAGE

microscopic VERY SMALL, ALMOST INVISIBLE TO THE HUMAN EYE

optic nerve THE GROUP OF NERVE FIBERS THAT PASS SIGNALS FROM THE RETINA AT THE BACK OF EACH EYE TO THE BRAIN

perceive TO NOTICE SOMETHING OR SOMEONE BY USING SIGHT, SOUND, TOUCH, TASTE, OR SMELL

pixel ONE OF THE TINY DOTS OF LIGHT THAT MAKE UP AN IMAGE ON A COMPUTER OR TELEVISION SCREEN

pupil THE SMALL, DARK OPENING IN THE CENTER OF THE EYE. LIGHT PASSES THROUGH THE PUPIL INTO THE EYE

radius A DISTANCE FROM A CENTRAL POINT

receiver SOMETHING OR SOMEONE THAT TAKES OR IS GIVEN SOMETHING

reflect THROW BACK (HEAT, LIGHT, OR SOUND) WITHOUT ABSORBING IT

retina THE AREA AT THE BACK OF THE EYE THAT RECEIVES LIGHT AND SENDS PICTURES OF WHAT THE EYE SEES TO THE BRAIN

sonic RELATED TO SOUND

sound wave THE FORM THAT SOUND TAKES WHEN IT PASSES THROUGH AIR OR WATER

stereoscopic THE PERCEPTION OF OBJECTS AS THREE-DIMENSIONAL

ultrasonic A SOUND TOO HIGH FOR HUMANS TO HEAR

FURTHER INFORMATION

WEBSITES

www.bbc.com/education/topics/z3nnb9q
VIDEO CLIPS ABOUT LIGHT AND SOUND

kidshealth.org/en/kids/ears.html and kidshealth.org/en/kids/eyes.html
TWO LINKS TO A WEBSITE THAT EXPLAINS HOW YOUR EYES AMD EARS WORK

https://www.dkfindout.com/uk/science/
INFORMATION TO IMPROVE YOUR KNOWLEDGE OF LIGHT AND SOUND

https://ed.ted.com/series/?series=superhero-science
AUTHOR JOY LIN'S TED ED VIDEOS ABOUT SCIENCE AND SUPERHEROES

BOOKS

Mind Webs: Light and Sound BY ANNA CLAYBOURNE (WAYLAND, 2015)

Science in a Flash: Light AND *Science in a Flash: Sound*
BY GEORGIA AMSON-BRADSHAW (FRANKLIN WATTS, 2017)

Science Makers: Making with Light AND *Science Makers: Making with Sound*
BY ANNA CLAYBOURNE (WAYLAND, 2018)

Science in Infographics: Light and Sound BY JON RICHARDS (WAYLAND, 2017)

EVERY EFFORT HAS BEEN MADE BY THE PUBLISHERS TO ENSURE THAT THE WEBSITES
IN THIS BOOK ARE SUITABLE FOR CHILDREN, THAT THEY ARE OF THE HIGHEST
EDUCATIONAL VALUE, AND THAT THEY CONTAIN NO INAPPROPRIATE OR OFFENSIVE
MATERIAL. HOWEVER, BECAUSE OF THE NATURE OF THE INTERNET, IT IS IMPOSSIBLE
TO GUARANTEE THAT THE CONTENTS OF THESE SITES WILL NOT BE ALTERED. WE
STRONGLY ADVISE THAT INTERNET ACCESS IS SUPERVISED BY A RESPONSIBLE ADULT.

INDEX